WOMEN, LIFE, FREEDOM

McCourtney Institute for Democracy

The Pennsylvania State University's McCourtney Institute for Democracy (http://democracyinstitute.la.psu.edu) was founded in 2012 as an interdisciplinary center for research, teaching, and outreach on democracy. The institute coordinates innovative programs and projects in collaboration with the Center for American Political Responsiveness and the Center for Democratic Deliberation.

Laurence and Lynne Brown Democracy Medal

The Laurence and Lynne Brown Democracy Medal recognizes outstanding individuals, groups, and organizations that produce exceptional innovations to further democracy in the United States or around the world. In even-numbered years, the medal spotlights practical innovations, such as new institutions, laws, technologies, or movements that advance the cause of democracy. Awards given in odd-numbered years highlight advances in democratic theory that enrich philosophical conceptions of democracy or empirical models of democratic behavior, institutions, or systems.

WOMEN, LIFE, FREEDOM

OUR FIGHT FOR HUMAN RIGHTS AND EQUALITY IN IRAN

NASRIN SOTOUDEH

TRANSLATED BY PARISA SARANJ
FOREWORD BY JEFF KAUFMAN

CORNELL UNIVERSITY PRESS
Ithaca and London

Thanks to generous funding from the McCourtney Institute for Democracy at Pennsylvania State University, the ebook editions of this book are available as open access volumes through the Cornell Open initiative.

First published 2023 by Cornell University Press

Librarians: A CIP catalog record for this book is available from the Library of Congress.

Library of Congress Control Number: 2023941779

ISBN 978-1-5017-7610-6 (paperback)
ISBN 978-1-5017-7611-3 (epub)
ISBN 978-1-5017-7612-0 (pdf)

Contents

Foreword

Nelson Mandela said, "No one truly knows a nation until one has been inside its jails." Nasrin Sotoudeh knows her nation too well.

On a warm June evening in 2018, Iranian human rights attorney Nasrin Sotoudeh and her activist husband, Reza Khandan, had a Skype call on their cellphone while strolling through a Tehran park. On the other end of that conversation, 6,000 miles away in New York City, was another couple: my wife, Marcia Ross, and I. We discussed our children, the documentary about Nasrin that we were producing, the possible effects of the recent withdrawal of the United States from the Iran nuclear deal, and Nasrin's work representing women protesting Iran's mandatory hijab laws. Nasrin and Reza were, as usual, in surprisingly good spirits.

The next day, Nasrin was arrested and sent to Evin Prison. She had been there before, from 2010 to 2013, charged with "conspiring to harm state security" and banned from working as a lawyer or leaving the country for twenty years. This time, she was sentenced to decades in prison and dozens of lashes on charges of inciting corruption and prostitution, disrupting public order, propaganda against the state, and collusion against national security. In other words: advocating for human rights in the Islamic Republic of Iran.

Two months later, Reza was arrested on similar charges. He was sentenced to six years in prison, but he was released on bail after 111 days to care for their children.

Nasrin was imprisoned for over three years. That included a forty-six-day hunger strike at the height of the pandemic to demand the release of political prisoners from Iran's notoriously overcrowded and unsanitary prisons. Gravely ill, she received a medical furlough in July 2021 because of a serious heart condition complicated by COVID-19.

Since her release, Nasrin and Reza have been threatened repeatedly with reimprisonment. Their bank accounts were frozen and their daughter has been harassed and interrogated by the authorities. They live each day knowing they could be sent back to prison at any time.

It is a heavy price to pay for loving one's country, and Nasrin shows no sign of backing down.

Nasrin was born in 1963 to a devout Muslim family in Langarud, a small city on the southern coast of the Caspian

Sea. Her parents raised their children to respect people of all faiths and backgrounds, and those values have defined her life.

Disregarding official ire, she has regularly given pro bono legal representation to religious and ethnic minorities who face discrimination in education, employment, and other basic civil rights. She has been a formidable advocate for women, children, journalists, artists, and nonviolent opposition figures in court, in public demonstrations, and in the media. A leading critic of capital punishment (Iran has the second-highest rate of executions in the world), in 2013, she cofounded a campaign called Step-by-Step to Stop the Death Penalty.

She has also been a fierce critic of Iran's mandatory hijab laws, which were the focus of the 2018 Girls of Revolution Street protests, and recent nationwide demonstrations following the death in custody of twenty-two-year-old Mahsa (Jina) Amini days after she was violently arrested by Iran's "morality" police. Nasrin understands the universal application of this kind of oppression and has expressed solidarity with reproductive rights advocates in the US. "The compulsory hijab law isn't just about controlling women's bodies," she said. "It's about controlling our ability to think for ourselves. This ensnares both sexes."

I first heard about Nasrin while making a film with Amnesty International about the persecution of the Baha'i Faith in Iran. She was spoken of with awe and affection by people touched by her work defending the defenseless in

Iran. As Nasrin said a few years ago, "Because we are all Iranians, we all suffer common pains. Our rights are systematically violated, although the rights of Baha'is are violated more than most."

That ability to see our common humanity and challenge repression in all forms is why Nasrin has often been called "the Nelson Mandela of Iran."

In 2016, Marcia and I contacted Nasrin through mutual friends to ask if she'd be interested in a documentary about her life and work. It was a troubling time, as politicians in the United States fanned anti-Islam anger, the Trump administration proposed a Muslim travel ban and a slow death watch began for the Joint Comprehensive Plan of Action to block Iran's path to a nuclear weapon. In Iran, hope for legal and social reforms promised by President Hassan Rouhani had turned to bitter disappointment over his two terms in office.

We wanted our film *Nasrin* to counter entrenched stereotypes and show that there is much to learn from Iran's people and culture. What better way to appreciate democracy and pluralism than to profile an individual like Nasrin Sotoudeh, who day after day puts her life at risk for those ideals?

Tragically, the march toward authoritarianism in the United States has grown faster and louder. That makes Nasrin's message and example more important than ever.

Many public figures can be privately disappointing. Not Nasrin. Over the course of making the film, campaigning for Nasrin's freedom, and working with Nasrin and Reza following her release, Marcia and I have gotten to know her as a good, albeit long-distance friend. She can be steely regarding social issues and the law (I wouldn't want to oppose her in court), but she is also incredibly warm and caring, with an infectious laugh that doesn't need a translation from Farsi to English.

One of the things we share is a love of the arts, which has often helped carry Nasrin through the pressures of her work. "I watch theater performances, I go to the cinema, and I frequently visit art exhibitions with my family," she said. "The arts are something I have always envied because they can do something that no other effort can. Art is the best way to take on tyranny. Art changes the rules of the game with tyrants."

Perhaps that is part of what prompted Nasrin's interest in the playwright, political prisoner, and the first president of the Czech Republic, Václav Havel. She recently wrote, "I've read Havel's *The Power of the Powerless* several times, and I read a biography of Havel after I came home from Qarchak Prison. His work leaves me in awe. When Havel analyzes the Czechoslovakia of his time, it's as if he's speaking about Iran."

Havel was a complicated combination of realist and optimist. That balance may have enabled him to persevere and break through incredible obstacles. Nasrin has that same compelling mix.

At the end of our documentary, Nasrin says, "The only way to establish tranquility, peace, and justice in our society is to demand our rights through nonviolent methods with persistence and tenacity. Without any costs, no society has achieved anything. Even though this movement hasn't yet achieved its desired results, it is an asset for our future steps."

Nasrin's depths as a person, her love of family, her passion for the arts, her physical and emotional courage, and the respect she innately shows everyone (even those who disrespect her) are just some of the reasons that I—and many others—hold her in such high esteem and hope that she will have a significant role in shaping the next phase of Iran's evolution.

—Jeff Kaufman, documentary director,
producer, and writer

WOMEN, LIFE,
FREEDOM

Introduction

A few days before Zahra was taken to be executed, she showed me a beautiful ballerina painting she had made in the Qarchak Women's Prison workshop for her young daughter. She had asked me with pride, "Isn't it beautiful?" And I, truly captivated by it, replied, "Yes, it's very beautiful." I still remember the painting vividly.

We were inmates in one of Iran's foulest and most overcrowded prisons. Qarchak was a converted industrial cow barn with an inadequate sewer system. My lungs were always filled with the smell of sewage. My cell was a small, windowless room with forty women and only twelve beds. We had to take turns sitting down to eat because there was not enough room for all of us to do so at once.

Zahra's story began with the murder of her husband. During our morning or evening walks in the prison yard, she would tell me how he subjected her and her sixteen-year-old

1

daughter to severe psychological and physical torture that made life a daily horror. In Iran, a man can easily get a divorce, but this is almost impossible for a woman. Divorced women also forfeit child custody. Zahra's daughter confessed in her diary that she had pulled the trigger and killed her father. She expressed no remorse, saying "she had escaped the hell he had created for them." Zahra's older children and her stepmother demanded legal retribution. The court, where all the judges were men, ultimately dismissed testimony about the father, and they blamed Zahra for her daughter's actions. They sentenced Zahra to death by hanging.

I was imprisoned with women like Zahra who experienced dark times with such grace. The cruel conditions force many prisoners and their families to lose their sense of humanity.

For a long time, my calling has been to defend political prisoners and those whose rights have been violated. In the 1970s, I read work by women like Shirin Ebadi and Mehrangiz Kar, whose writing awakened my enthusiasm and passion for an equitable society built on just laws. They had come of age before the 1979 Islamic Revolution and understood the world far better than I did. I was only fifteen years old during the revolution, and the extent of the emerging official misogyny had not yet overshadowed my life. Having witnessed changes in attitudes toward women since adolescence, I felt a tangled anger that I couldn't clearly express.

When I was twenty-one years old, I took an undergraduate law class in Islamic jurisprudence. The professor was a cleric who also taught at the university before the revolution and occasionally expressed opposition to the Islamic government. I asked him, "Why does the law consider blood money (*diyah*) for a woman to be half of that for a man?" This was one of the provisions in Iran's postrevolution Constitution. It meant that if a man unintentionally killed a man, he would have to pay blood money to the victim's family, but if he unintentionally killed a woman, only half of that amount would be awarded to hers. This was obviously demeaning to women. A cleric would have the answer, I thought. He responded with a kind of evasion, saying, "I don't know why. Ask those who have enacted these laws."

This was forty years ago. While my young mind was not yet fluent with concepts like activism, civil discourse, and human rights, I was unsatisfied with my professor's answer.

Around the same time, I traveled to Yazd with my best friend. We began to discuss how confused and upset we were by the new regime's treatment of women. She never allowed fear and caution to stop her from speaking the truth; she always spoke her mind. I mentioned the double standards that existed in family law. For example, in a divorce, a woman can have custody of her child only until the child is seven years old. This doesn't apply to men. In addition, a male child gets double his sisters' inheritance.

My friend, who had studied in America, suggested we teach other women about these inequalities. "Nasrin," she said, "let's write down all these unjust legal provisions; no need to explain, we'll just write down the exact wording of the law." She wanted us to make copies and distribute them among our friends. I'm embarrassed to say that I didn't take her suggestion seriously. I know better now, but I didn't think it could significantly influence anyone's thoughts.

Soon after that trip, I found an article by Shirin Ebadi. She was the first woman president of the Tehran city court and one of the first women judges in Iran. However, after the 1979 revolution, she was prevented from practicing as a lawyer until 1993. In that article, she wrote in simple and accessible language about the same legal discrimination that my best friend and I had discussed. She told women how the law systematically dismissed their rights. Later, on a cold winter morning, I went to Shirin Ebadi's law office for an interview commemorating International Women's Day and our friendship began.

At the same time, another remarkable woman challenged gender discrimination: the attorney and activist Mehrangiz Kar. She was a skillful writer who related the struggles young women faced in our unjust society. All these years later, I remember reading her story about how they couldn't even clap at music concerts or express themselves through words and dance. This soft-spoken but brave woman endured years of imprisonment and harassment by the Iranian authorities that ravaged her family and eventually led to her husband's death.

Those writings and discussions with my friend made an impression on me. I was about twenty-eight years old when

I realized that instead of simply questioning my professor, I should ask myself, "What should I do with my life?"

I decided to become a lawyer.

Excited and determined, I took the bar exam and passed in 1995, but I had to wait another seven years before I was permitted to practice law. To hold any official position in Iran, one's education and qualifications are never enough. There is a second process of selection known as *gozinesh* that evaluates a candidate's ideological beliefs. Matters such as religious beliefs—which have nothing to do with the position—are often assessed. When a candidate intends to practice law, the Iranian Bar Association is legally obligated to inform the Ministry of Intelligence, which in turn does a through background investigation.

Farideh Ghayrat, an attorney, women's rights activist, and spokesperson for the Association for the Defense of Prisoners' Rights helped me get my license. She repeatedly corresponded with the Ministry of Intelligence with incredible courage, exposing their meaningless excuses for my not passing the *gozinesh* evaluations. In a time when few dared to undertake to stand up to the ministry, I owe my career and all that followed to this woman.

Farideh was always concerned about women's rights and wrote numerous articles in various newspapers to challenge the misogynist laws. Besides her work as a spokesperson, she had been elected to the board of directors of the Iranian Bar Association; our interests crossed. Later, I had an internship with her. She taught me many principles about work ethic and persuasion that were, in many ways, even more important than the nuances of the laws and penal codes.

I was once working on a child abuse case that was not going anywhere. I had tried every legal path possible, but the presiding judge refused to consider the child's well-being. One day, particularly frustrated and angry, I went into the office and began complaining. "I expected more from you," Farideh said. What she told me next was the most crucial lesson of my life as a human rights lawyer. "When you are exhausted and cannot continue is exactly the time to be strong and push." My mentor taught me if I were tired, my opponent was too. "Be strong and push through," she recommended, and I listened. Soon, I won my case.

Fortunately, we were not alone. A few lawyers, such as Abdul-Karim Lahiji, defended political prisoners during this turbulent time. His work had begun during the previous regime, when the Shah cracked down on freedom of the press, workers' rights, and political activism, as well as persecuted human rights activists. Lahiji continued to do similar work for several years after the revolution. However, a sudden raid by revolutionary forces on the Lawyers Association forced him into hiding for a long time. Eventually, he left Iran. Once abroad, he contributed significantly to the legal field. Many well-known lawyers were detained during that raid, and the licenses of sixty-three human rights defense lawyers were illegally revoked. Among those whose licenses were invalidated were Gitie Pourfazel, a tireless advocate for women's rights, and Dariush Forouhar, a prominent leader of the revolution who, along with his wife, was murdered in 1998 by government agents. This coincided with the beginning of the horror stories in my country.

I started to practice law in 2003. I represented religious minorities such as Baha'is, ethnic minorities, especially Kurds, and many women and children who faced domestic abuse. I've also defended juveniles sentenced to death and worked with others to oppose the death penalty. I believe that human beings here, and in every country, deserve the right to freedom and dignified life.

Throughout history, women have long been the central figures of oppression.

In Iran, they have also been the central figures of change. In 2006, the One Million Signature Campaign delivered a petition to the Iranian Parliament to change the discriminatory laws against women. In 2017 and 2018, the Girls of Enghelab (Revolution) Street protests showed national opposition to this country's compulsory hijab laws. Many were violently arrested by the morality police and security forces, and I was the lawyer for some of these women.

There is a continual demand for social justice in Iran. The Women, Life, Freedom movement began in 2021 after the arrest and brutal killing of Mahsa Amini by the morality police. The dictatorship's response has been to tighten the noose on the Iranian people, and our women in custody and in prisons face the harshest violence. Children as young as nine have been gunned down. Young men who survived beatings were executed. Yet, we do not quit. We continue to pressure the government for basic rights and democratic change.

Silence is the enemy of human rights inside Iran and around the world. In my last few years in prison, I noticed how important social media and technology are in the fight against oppression. True change has to come from within, but the pressure and a good example from democratic countries can make an enormous difference. Iranian women have asked the international community for help righteously, respectfully, and peacefully. And there must be a global effort to honor their request. If not, what's happening in Afghanistan under Taliban rule will soon happen in Iran. As much as I resent having to make such a comparison, this is an inescapable truth.

In challenging times, I like to remember my aunt Anis. Fifty years ago, she was a teacher in a small town. Without a hijab and full of pride, she would stand in the middle of the town square and make speeches encouraging women to fight for their rights.

She loved her students, and their mothers would often go to her for personal advice. My aunt was never afraid to speak to their fathers and husbands if it could help these children in some way. One of my most vivid childhood memories is of my aunt standing up straight, hands in her pockets saying, "A woman should be able to reach her into own pockets." She was adamant about women being financially independent. That had a profound effect on me.

This and countless other stories like hers are told all over Iran, but they are nothing but a memory today. The reality now is the murder of Mahsa Amini, who lost her life for not covering herself in layers of clothes. The reality is the poisoning of schoolgirls with gas for daring to get an education. The reality is that women have endured over four decades of pain in this country. This is, for us, a physical, bodily experience. It's as real an aspect of life here as it could be.

People far away may turn their backs on these realities, hoping they are immune. However, if the monster of oppression has nested in one corner of the world, it doesn't mean it won't get up and move. No, it has already begun to prowl. The monster is hungry, and it dreams of taking over the world. We must overcome our fears, stand up to the beast, and look it in the eyes.

I want our children to see and be inspired by great women like my aunt. I don't want her to live only as a memory, as a dream. That's why I will try everything I can to give the women of Iran the society they deserve.

Pennsylvania State University's McCourtney Institute for Democracy has asked me to write an essay explaining my work. Even though I am honored, I know this can't be about me. It will be possible only if I talk about the work of other people and groups in Iran. In fact, every time the rights of women, children, or minorities were undermined, I merely provided legal representation for the activists who fought for them. My efforts have always depended on other civil and human rights activists. For example, I represented various women's rights activists in an attempt to overturn or reduce the harsh punishment they would receive. Another example is my work for juveniles sentenced to death for crimes they had committed at a young age. I share concerns with colleagues in this struggle. Our sole purpose is to end the severe abuse happening in our society. I simply contributed to the cause with the tools of my profession.

Looking back, I realize there were many occasions when I could reduce my clients' sentences and sometimes help free innocent people. Tragically, after repeated brutal pressure from the government, the work of feminist groups and the human rights attorneys who defended them (including myself) have been almost completely shut down. However, good people are harvesting the seeds we have sown, just as we did with the activists who came before us.

Forty-four years ago, the Iranian people hoped for freedom in the revolution that swept away the Shah. They were lied to and betrayed. The government of Ayatollah Khomeini stripped away their civil and political rights. They did this with a self-righteousness that comes when a few governing men are convinced they are God's representatives on earth, and their version of religion gradually slithered its way into citizens' personal lives.

Women bore the brunt of the social and political repression. Almost all of their civil rights were taken away from them. The right to divorce, custody of their children, freedom to choose hijab, equal inheritance, and protection from polygamy—which had slightly improved under the previous regime—were completely abolished. This was despite the Islamic Republic government's promise of a new country where men and women were equal. Unfortunately, women lacked the political awareness to recognize the depth of the problem, and even though the new institution saw them as nothing but sex objects, they had to compromise and—ignoring the compulsory hijab law—focus on fighting for their civil rights, including the right to education and employment.

Eventually, women realized they could not claim civil rights unless they could claim control of their bodies. Thus began civil disobedience against wearing the mandatory hijab in public.

Out of this awareness, various movements surfaced, such as the Stop Stoning Forever Campaign, the One Million Signature Campaign, and My Stealthy Freedom (White Wednesdays). From these, a spontaneous and grassroots movement called the Girls of Revolution Street was born. Women of all ages publicly waved their headscarves on a stick. No amount of oppression—jailing, torture, death—can stop the generational call for our rights.

Today, I hope to record a small part of what has happened. I must discuss women's rights in Iran and the laws concerning the activists who challenge those rights. As a lawyer who can never freely offer a critical review of the law in her country, I am delighted to be given this platform for such a close analysis. My goal is to answer three questions:

1. What does the Constitution say about the mandatory hijab, and why do women oppose those laws?
2. What methods do women use to oppose compulsory hijab laws, and what challenges do they face?
3. What politics have been behind the sentences against the women opposing hijab laws, and do they carry legal weight?

I will approach answering the above questions from four directions:

1. Discussing the mandatory hijab laws in the Constitution.
2. Recounting the reasons behind harassment and imprisonment of women opposing hijab laws.
3. Explaining my defense of the women opposing hijab laws.
4. Analyzing the texts of the judicial verdicts against women opposing hijab laws.

1

The History of Compulsory Hijab

Following the 1979 revolution, a wave of Islamization swept through Iran. This wave, encompassing every dimension of society, had a central target: women's rights. The extremist Islamists advocated restrictive new laws that claimed the old laws represented the previous regime and were a sign of Westernization.

In a November 1978 interview while in France, Ayatollah Ruhollah Khomeini said women had "the freedom to choose or to be chosen, the freedom to educate themselves while working and engaging in any kind of economic activity." But when he returned to Iran in February 1979, after the January abdication of King Reza Pahlavi, Khomeini's words changed, and his true intentions quickly became apparent.

In the face of this extremism, a variety of intellectual currents remained silent and even found it convenient to do so. Some opponents of the Shah pressured them to wear the hijab and obey so-called moral commands issued within the domain of male-dominated households. The hijab, or veiling, is a strict dress code, punishable by fines or imprisonment, mandating that all females over nine must cover their hair (usually with a headscarf) and dress in a chador or modest clothes.

Twenty-four days after the revolution's victory, on February 4, 1979, this issue of compulsory hijab was raised by Ayatollah Khomeini in a speech delivered among theology students in the holy city of Qom. He stated, "Islamic women should appear with Islamic hijab to not degrade themselves. Women are still working in government offices in the same way as before the revolution. Women should change their appearance . . . I have been informed that women appear naked in government offices, which is against Sharia law. Women can participate in social activities but with hijab" (*Kayhan* newspaper, February 17, 1979).

I was sixteen years old when Ayatollah Khomeini's words were in the headlines and every conversation. One afternoon, our next-door neighbor visited my mother, and I overheard her saying, "I feel insulted." She was a working woman.

These statements by Ayatollah Khomeini also sparked widespread protests. As government institutions began to restrict the entry of unveiled employees and visitors, many women took to the streets on March 8, International Women's Day. Over the following days, they demonstrated against compulsory hijab, chanting, "Freedom is universal, neither

14

Eastern nor Western," and, "We did not have a revolution to go backward."

The first slogan was in response to the dominant discourse of the time, which had cast a shadow over Iranian society. It regarded any discussion of women's rights as discourse inspired by the West, and since revolutionary forces considered the fight against Western symbols as one of their primary objectives, they also opposed women's rights.

As a woman, as someone who has studied the law, and as a human rights activist, I can tell you that it is a woman's certain right to decide for herself what she wants or does not want to wear. If a woman chooses to be veiled, so be it. It is her right. The same must apply if a woman chooses not to be veiled. However, the compulsory hijab law isn't just about controlling women's bodies. It's really about controlling our ability to think for ourselves. This ensnares both sexes.

Women continued to gather in demonstrations in front of the Ministry of Foreign Affairs, the Technical College of the University of Tehran, and the Prime Minister's Office. However, the biggest gathering of women had taken place on February 8, 1979, in front of the courthouse, where Homa Nategh, a professor of history at the University of Tehran, addressed the crowd. "We are not against hijab; we are against its imposition." These protestors, estimated to be 15,000 people on that date, went from the courthouse to the Prime Minister's Office to express their opposition to the compulsory hijab (*Ettela'at* newspaper, February 19, 1979). Likewise, on

February 17, 1979, *Kayhan* newspaper reported, "Various groups of women have taken to the streets in northern and central Tehran to express their opinions about hijab. . . . The demonstration occurred while continuous snowfall started in the early morning hours."

Sayyid Mahmoud Taleghani, a prominent and supposedly moderate cleric, responded to this public outcry by stating in an interview with *Ettela'at* that the hijab is an explicit command in the Quran. He said Islam intends to preserve the dignity of women, and this dress code is one of the Islamic and Iranian commands. He said, "There is no need to discuss the compulsory hijab."

Soon afterward, on March 12, 1979, Ayatollah Khomeini supported Mahmoud Taleghani's statement. That's how the protestors, who believed they would achieve their demand for noncompulsory hijab, realized that their movement had, for the moment, been stopped.

On April 1, 1979, eligible Iranian citizens went to the polls in a referendum about the legitimacy of the emerging system. According to official results, 98.2 percent voted in favor of the Islamic Republic.

A spring morning in the schoolyard during recess sums up my experience of those tense months. I was chatting with a few classmates when a friend approached us and said, "It's over. Hijab is now mandatory." I was in eleventh grade, and my future was ahead of me; yet my world collapsed. I felt buried alive and wondered how to make my way out.

After the referendum, Ayatollah Khomeini remained silent. During his hiatus, on July 5, 1979, government offices officially began preventing women from appearing without hijab at work. Once again, women protested, but not as extensively as before because they were met with severe suppression and arrests.

Enactment of Compulsory Hijab Law

Before the enactment of the 1979 Constitution, Ayatollah Khomeini approved—illegally—the compulsory hijab law and deprived women of their social rights, including the right to work based on compliance with the Islamic hijab. Four years later, on August 9, 1983, the compulsory hijab officially became one of the articles in the Islamic Penal Code approved by the representatives of the Parliament.

According to Article 102, Clause 1, of the Islamic Penal Code passed in 1983: "Women who appear in public places and thoroughfares without observing the Islamic hijab shall be sentenced to imprisonment from ten days to two months or fined."

Since the Islamic Penal Code was initially enacted as an experiment, it underwent periodic review every few years and was reapproved by the Parliament with the implemented amendments. The phrases related to compulsory hijab mentioned above were repeated verbatim in the latest version of the Islamic Penal Code, which was approved by the Parliament in 2013, specifically in Clause 638 of the same law.

Some Iranian women have been willing to pay the fines stipulated in this article or even endure imprisonment for not observing hijab. However, the Islamic Penal Code has enacted another article, Article 639, which states, "Individuals shall be sentenced to imprisonment from one to ten years for inciting people to corruption or providing the means for it."

It is important to mention this point when talking about the Girls of Revolution Street in 2017 and 2018. The women who participated by removing their headscarves, an act intended by them as civil disobedience, would ultimately face the provisions of Article 638 of the Islamic Penal Code. However, in subsequent stages, depending on the circumstances of the accused, the attributed charges, and the judge's interpretation of "taking off hijab," would fall under the provisions of Article 639. This links a woman removing her headscarf in public to an act of prostitution or encouraging people to commit immorality or prostitution. It calls for sentences of one to ten years in prison.

Personal Experiences

Despite enacting the disgraceful law on compulsory hijab, the Islamic Republic obscured its approach to this law. For years, the regime refrained from acknowledging the mandatory hijab in international forums. In response to outside inquiries about the coercion of women to wear hijab, it claimed that Iranian women voluntarily accept this dress as part of Iranian culture. Although blatantly false, many people believed veiling had been an Iranian tradition for years. In fact, human rights activists and journalists who came to Iran repeatedly asked me the truth about hijab. When I informed them that not observing hijab is a crime according to the Islamic Penal Code, they were often astonished. I had to show them the text to prove I was not lying.

The Islamic Republic's attack on women did not stop there.

Relying on the police force, the regime used forms of violence that went beyond the boundaries of the law. For example, many women and girls on the streets were harassed by police officers under the pretext of improper hijab. These women wore a headscarf, but the way the scarves were styled did not meet the officers' approval. Therefore, these women were considered unveiled. The officers, based on their personal interpretations and preferences, took the initiative to arrest and physically assault women whom they deemed *bad hijab* or "improperly veiled." The term did not even exist in the law but has caused widespread harm.

Imagine the terror of living your everyday life and not knowing when you will be targeted. You could be on your way to school, work, or a shop when randomly stopped by the morality police, who inspect your clothes. At any of these points, you can be harassed, arrested, and taken to prison.

I have represented numerous women who were arrested for allegedly not adhering to Iran's compulsory hijab laws, some who were arrested simply for wearing a colorful headscarf or a long floral skirt.

The government also pursued initiatives to control women's bodies through extralegal means. For example, according to the law, taking and publishing photos without a hijab was not a crime, but no woman was allowed to have an identification card or passport that displayed such images. Additionally, after receiving Italy's 2008 Human Rights Prize, I recorded my acceptance speech in my office. In 2010, in addition to a sentence of imprisonment and work prohibition, I was personally convicted and fined 50,000 tomans for that video. I never agreed to pay the fine. I was ready to refuse payment if judicial authorities requested it and tell them I would rather go to prison. Eventually, the judicial system gave up on that sentence.

Another form of extralegal pressure on women was the mandatory use of chador in certain government facilities, including prisons. Female prisoners were required to wear the body-length covering traditionally only worn by devout women. For years, I was aware of this compulsion in prisons, and I had witnessed numerous times the mandatory garb when visiting my clients. During those visits, I promised to not submit to the burden of wearing a chador if I ever found myself imprisoned.

The compulsion of wearing a chador in prison posed a significant challenge after my arrest in 2010. When I refused to wear it in detention, I was threatened that I would not be taken to the courthouse unless I complied. The implication was that I would remain indefinitely in solitary confinement. "It doesn't matter," I responded. My nonchalant attitude must have worked because they took me to the courthouse anyway.

The main challenge, which continued for one-and-a-half years after my arrest, arose during the weekly visits. When I was held in Ward 209 at the Intelligence Detention Center, twice I was denied my biweekly visitation sessions with my husband and children because I refused to wear a chador. Later in May 2011, I was transferred to the general ward. There, I continued to challenge wearing the chador during visitation hours. At first, it cost me a few visits, but soon the authorities succumbed to my constant opposition, and other female prisoners also began to abandon the chador.

Unfortunately, that was not the end of it. After four months, the prison authorities made wearing the chador mandatory again. They stipulated that visitors to the infirmary or the visitation hall must wear it. As a result, women who refused were deprived of receiving medical services and visitation rights. I remember one woman sentenced to three years for peacefully protesting. Because she resisted, she was prohibited from going to the infirmary until the end of her sentence. She was almost sixty years old, and despite needing medical care, she still refused to comply. Similarly, I was indefinitely denied family visits because I was not willing under any circumstances to bend to their demands either.

From August to October 2011, after two months of not being allowed to see my young children, the prison authorities agreed to resume my visitation rights. I was allowed to appear without a chador, separated from the other prisoners in the visitation hall.

The regime continued to play psychological games with the political prisoners. When the news of the ban on my visitation rights became public, it highlighted how female prisoners were forced to wear the chador. In response to a reporter's question about this issue, the deputy director of the judiciary said, "Forcing female prisoners to wear the chador is an insult to the chador," which was an affront to the women who refused to wear it. He then falsely claimed that the head of the judiciary had issued an order to abolish the compulsory chador for female inmates (*Vatan Emrooz* newspaper, Thursday, 30 Shahrivar 1390).

The Evin Prison warden, a man called Suri, ignored the judiciary and made his own rules about women's attire. He ordered a special chador for female prisoners. It was a bright yellow fabric with elastic in four places covering the hands and the feet. The elastic rings that went around the wrists and ankles were meant to prevent the chador from slipping.

Rules like these are why I say inmates are in the small prison, and the rest of our citizens are in the big prison.

On the occasion of Nowruz, the Persian New Year, in the spring of 2012, the interim head of the prison visited the women's ward as part of the customary New Year's visit. Mahvash Shahriari Sabet, one of the leaders of the Baha'i community in Iran, had been sentenced to ten years in prison simply for practicing her faith. Calmly, she addressed the interim chief and asked him to finally end the compulsion of prisoners to wear the chador. The prison chief said he had no problem with it, but the matter needed to be discussed with higher authorities. He assured Mahvash he would follow up and let her know.

After a short period, the request was accepted. The women prisoners were happy. It was a very small request, but it was significant given the hurdles the prisoners had had to overcome.

Since then, wearing a chador in prison has been optional for women. However, the bigger issue of the hijab in Iranian society remains. Now, with the Women, Life, Freedom movement that followed the tragic death of Mahsa Amini, women in all parts of the country—inside and outside the prisons—are striving to abolish the compulsory hijab.

2

The Girls of Revolution Street

The Beginnings

Although Iranian women had been undertaking scattered actions for years to protest against compulsory hijab, it was a specific incident that led to the start of the Girls of Revolution Street movement. It all began with a thirty-two-year-old woman named Vida Movahed.

On December 27, 2017, a video surfaced on social media showing a young woman standing on a utility box at the Enghelab Street and Vozara Avenue intersection. She had tied her white headscarf to a stick and was waving it gracefully. Almost a month after the video was released, there was still no news about this woman whose identity remained unknown. My husband Reza and I were concerned about what had happened to her and decided to visit the location.

Through inquiries with local shopkeepers and passersby, we learned that this woman had a nine-month-old baby and had done this three times before. Additionally, we discovered that she had an open case with the Guidance Court, which handles hijab-related offenses. I posted on my Facebook page about my inquiry and went to the relevant courthouse the following day to see what I could discover. I was not there as a lawyer but as a concerned citizen. There, I learned the brave woman's name, Vida Movahed, and that she would soon be released on bail. By this time, the public had begun learning about her and recognizing the significance of her actions.

On February 29, 2018, the second Girl of Revolution Street, Narges Hosseini, climbed onto the same utility box. This time the streets of Tehran were covered in snow.

Many of us were delighted with the continuation of this protest. Schools, including my children's, were closed because of the heavy snowfall. My mother-in-law was visiting our house. My teenage daughter, who was actively following the issue of compulsory hijab at that time, showed me a photo of Narges Hosseini on her phone. My mother-in-law and I looked at the picture with joy and smiled. Despite being a traditional woman, my mother-in-law is very open-minded. She knew about my visit to Revolution Street and was dedicated to this issue. Her joy quickly disappeared, however, and she seemed concerned. "Won't it be dangerous for you?" I assured her that I was safe.

A few hours after that conversation, my mobile phone rang. A young girl introduced herself as Narges Hosseini's sister and said that Narges had been arrested. It turned out that Narges had gotten word to her sister that she wanted me to legally represent her. I scheduled a meeting at my office, and work began.

After Narges, other women, including Azam Jangravi and Maryam Shariatmadari, repeated the protest. However, the police forcibly pulled them down. The utility box was approximately one-and-a-half meters high. Maryam Shariatmadari's foot caught on a sharp object, causing a small wound. As soon as these women were arrested, they were transferred to Qarchak Prison, one of the most notorious prisons in Iran.

Many women removed their headscarves publicly in different parts of the city. They expressed solidarity with the Girls of Revolution Street by sharing their pictures on social media.

I represented four of them: Narges Hosseini, Maryam Shariatmadari, Shaparak Shajari Zadeh, and another woman who did not wish to disclose the details of the arrest, harassment, and abuse she experienced at the hands of the police. And, of course, before I could complete my work as a lawyer in these cases, I was arrested on June 13, 2018, for defending these women.

The women's movement in Iran, striving for forty years to protect our rights through dialogue, was now experiencing a change in strategy. We were standing up—literally and symbolically—against the control over women's bodies. We were returning to the starting point of our historical struggle with the Iranian government. We were turning back the pages of history to the year 1979 when the Islamic government ordered women to observe the hijab in their workplaces, or else they would be dismissed.

Indeed, in recent years, we have witnessed how dictatorships in the Middle East (and countries worldwide) have reduced women's rights and their bodies to mere instruments of their rule. That is why democracy is impossible without realizing women's rights.

The Girls of Revolution Street

Narges Hosseini

On February 29, 2018, Narges Hosseini was arrested while standing on top of a utility box with her scarf hanging from a stick she was waving. Narges was a graduate student of sociology from a conservative but supportive family. I, along with Arash Keykhosravi, a colleague, took on her legal representation. I have always worked on civil and human rights cases with other lawyers so that defending my cases would not be disrupted if I were arrested.

Narges called me from Qarchak Prison, one of Iran's most notorious women's prisons. Overcrowded and unsanitary, it houses over 1,400 women, many convicted of violent crimes.

In years to come, I would also find myself at Qarchak, suffering from a heart condition and a harsh case of COVID-19.

Over the phone, my first impression of her was of a strong and confident young woman. Right off the bat, she wanted me to know that she was not remorseful and under no circumstances willing to repent. She kept this attitude throughout her trial.

As soon as we arrived at Qarchak Prison, we delivered a power of attorney to Narges and began the process of defending her. At the same time, we planned the defense and divided the work between us; we tried to convince the relevant judicial authority to reduce the bail amount. Before then, the appropriate court had issued a bail amount of 500 million tomans, which was quite high. Plus, Narges could not afford it. The court reduced the bail to 60 million tomans. A philanthropist I knew and trusted donated that money to support the protest against compulsory hijab.

After unnecessary delays and judicial gamesmanship, everything required for Narges' temporary release was eventually submitted, and she was released from Qarchak Prison. The charges brought against her were as follows:

1. Encouraging corruption by unveiling the hijab in public view.
2. Committing an unlawful act.
3. Appearing in public places without observing the proper Islamic hijab.

The punishment for the first charge, according to the law, is imprisonment ranging from two to ten years. The second accusation could carry a prison sentence ranging from ten days to two months or up to seventy-four lashes. The punishment for the third accusation is imprisonment ranging from ten days to two months or a fine of 5,000 to 50,000 tomans.

Narges' action, even though we disagreed with the law it was based on, was at most in line with the provisions of Subsection (c) of Article 638 of the Islamic Penal Code, which corresponds to her third accusation. However, contrary to all common principles, the respective judge considered three criminal charges for a single act, which could have resulted in up to ten years of imprisonment.

Defense arguments. At the prosecutor's office, the magistrate issued the order of criminality against the defendant in less than twenty-four hours. In practice, the entry of the defense lawyer into the case was not allowed, thus depriving the client of a legal defense.

Defending her actions, Narges Hosseini stated that her motivation was to protest against the lack of women's right to choose their clothing, and she deliberately chose a crowded area of the city so that more people could witness her protest. She mentioned that the choice of a white scarf and the location of the electrical box were in solidarity with Vida Movahed, the first Girl of Revolution Street.

When the charges were read to her and she was asked about her defense, she said, "As a woman, I demand the right to choose. I hate force and coercion of any kind. And I admit that I took off my scarf and stood on the utility box" (quoted from the judicial case).

It should be noted that a young man was also arrested for filming Narges, but he was released after a few hours. He was one of many men, like my husband Reza, who put themselves at risk by supporting the Girls of Revolution Street and women's rights in Iran.

Our defense arguments were based on a thorough reading of the Constitution and more progressive analyses than the jurisprudential foundations of the "religious hijab":

1. The Constitution emphasizes the principle of equality between men and women, including the right to choose clothing. Therefore, women can choose their attire and should not be forced. This principle of equality undercuts the regime's position and actions.

2. The legislator's intention regarding the "religious hijab" is not merely about covering the hair. It is about observing a form of hijab that does not undermine public morals. In other words, hijab is a socially defined concept that is contextual and dependent on time and place. The defendant chose to stand on the electrical box with winter clothing on a snowy day to express her opposition to the government's forced imposition of wearing a headscarf.

3. Other religious opinions that did not consider covering the hair obligatory were mentioned. The combination of the Constitution and these diverse religious opinions in Narges' defense was for several reasons. Firstly, the term "Sharia hijab" has been left undefined in the law and, over the years, citizens have attempted to reach a consensus with the government on its limited interpretation, arguing that Sharia hijab does not solely refer to covering the hair. On the other hand, the government has tried to expand the definition of hijab through a broader interpretation, encompassing any attire preferred by the relevant authorities. In the proposed legislation, we, as lawyers, sought to narrow down the interpretation of Sharia hijab in favor of the defendant, given the ambiguity in the law. It is worth noting that interpreting laws in favor of the accused is a recognized legal principle in judicial systems worldwide.

Secondly, in Iran's judicial system, it is very common for judges to refer to religious opinions for various reasons. We also took this approach because our objective was the defendant's dignified freedom.

In response to the judge's argument that hijab is a matter of culture and law and has been recommended to preserve public morality, Narges calmly asked the judge, "Why should I bear all the costs of this public morality?"

At the end of the defense, we requested a fair judgment acquitting their client.

Court verdict. Branch 1089 of Criminal Court 2, Judiciary Complex of Ershad Tehran, presided over by Judge Ali Asghar Mousavi Kanti, issued a verdict in case number 9609972124401973 dated April 3, 2018, as follows, sentencing the defendant, Ms. Narges Hosseini:

Regarding the criminal complaint filed by the 21st District Court of Tehran with case number 9610432123008968 against the accused, Ms. Narges Hosseini, represented by Ms. Nasrin Studeh and Mr. Arash Kikhosravi, the following charges were brought against her:

1. Encouraging corruption by unveiling the hijab in public view.
2. Committing a forbidden act.
3. Appearing in public places without observing the religious hijab.

It should be noted that on 1/30/2018, on Enghelab Street in Tehran, the accused publicly unveiled her hijab (removed her headscarf) and stood on an electric utility box, placing her headscarf on a stick, as evidenced by solid images in the case file. She stated her motive as protesting the mandatory nature of the hijab and explained the reason for choosing this location. She was also seen with a white headscarf amid the crowd and the presence of a previously arrested individual on Enghelab Street. However, based on the contents of the case file, and the statements of the accused, it is clear that this act was not a random or spontaneous incident merely motivated by an objection to the mandatory hijab. Instead, it was a coordinated and organized act aimed at encouraging people to engage in similar behavior as the accused, with its reflection in Islamic society and the repetition of this act by other women supporting such encouragement.

Furthermore, there is a distinction between a woman's appearance in society without observing the religious hijab and the accused's actions. In addition to unveiling the hijab and removing the headscarf, the accused stood at an elevated location and raised a white headscarf to eradicate the stigma associated with such acts and normalize them in Islamic society. This constitutes a clear example of encouraging corruption. Considering the statements and defenses of the accused's lawyers, claiming that "a woman without a headscarf does not constitute a violation of the religious hijab" and "no one has the right to violate the legitimate freedom of the people, even with the enactment of laws, and mandatory hijab in public places is contrary to the ninth principle of the Constitution."[1]

---

1. Ninth Principle: In the Islamic Republic of Iran, freedom, independence, and territorial integrity are inseparable, and their preservation is the duty

Firstly, according to eminent jurists' fatwas, covering all body parts except the face and hands is obligatory. Therefore, unveiling women's hijab and not wearing a headscarf in public places and streets has religious sanctity.

Secondly, assuming that the hijab is not mandatory according to the opinion of some jurists, it does not mean that the unveiling of the hijab is not contrary to religious principles and does not constitute a violation.

Thirdly, according to Articles 2 and 3 of the Islamic Penal Code enacted in 2013, any behavior, whether an act or an omission, for which a punishment is specified in the law is considered a crime, and penal laws apply to all individuals who commit crimes within the jurisdiction of Iran. Therefore, as long as the law has not been repealed and remains in force, the offender will be deserving of punishment. Considering the entirety of the case, the report of the law enforcement officers, the observation of the photo related to the discovery of the hijab by the accused in the case, the confession of the accused to the principle of committing the

---

of the government and all individuals of the nation. No individual, group, or authority has the right to use freedom to undermine the political, cultural, economic, and military independence or territorial integrity of Iran, even under the pretext of preserving independence and territorial integrity. Legitimate freedoms, even with the enactment of laws and regulations, cannot be violated.

act during the investigations by the law enforcement agency and the court, and the lack of valid justifications by the accused and her defense lawyers, along with other evidence and indications present in the case, the guilt of the accused is established and certain. Furthermore, since the accused has committed an act that, according to the issued indictment, carries multiple criminal titles, the court, based on Article 131 of the Islamic Penal Code enacted in 2013, which states that in crimes punishable by *ta'zir* (discretionary punishment), if the unitary behavior has multiple criminal titles, the offender shall be subject to the most severe punishment, sentences the accused to a term of twenty-four months of discretionary imprisonment, based on Clause B of Article 639 of the Islamic Penal Code, Book Five, *Ta'zirat*, enacted in 1996. However, considering the deterrent nature of suspended sentences and the presence of specified conditions for the suspension of the sentence, including the absence of a prior criminal record, and considering the announcement of the completion of the execution of a three-month imprisonment term, based on Article 46 of the Islamic Penal Code enacted in 2013, the court suspends the execution of the remaining term of imprisonment, amounting to five years. It is reminded that if the convicted person commits one of the intentional crimes resulting in *hadd* (prescribed punishment), *qisas* (retribution), *diya* (blood money), or *ta'zir* of the seventh degree during the suspension period, in addition to the execution of the punishment for the recent crime, the suspended punishment will also be enforced; otherwise, the suspended sentence will become ineffective. The issued verdict is in-person and subject to reconsideration within twenty days after notification in the Tehran Provincial Court of Appeals.

Analysis of the issued verdict. According to this ruling, the judge considered Narges' actions incitement to corruption and indecency. As a result, the defendant was sentenced to two years of imprisonment, with three months deemed executable and the execution of the remaining sentence suspended for five years. Although with time served, we were grateful that Narges had minimal prison time, this verdict had significant problems. These included the fact that the judge listed three charges for merely a single act of "civil disobedience," which is not logically compatible with any legal reasoning. The judge's argument in considering three charges against the defendant is a presumption of intent based on the judge's perception of the defendant's behavior. In a section of the ruling, the judge mentions that this act was entirely coordinated and organized to encourage people to engage in conduct similar to that of the accused and then concludes that this act was coordinated with other individuals.

The fact that the defendant intended to carry out this act of civil disobedience is indeed a point that she repeatedly emphasized and is also a characteristic of civil disobedience itself. However, in her defense, the defendant often mentioned that she made this decision personally and engaged in this act solely as a protest against the mandatory hijab.

On the other hand, this verdict is contrary to the principles of Articles 20 and 29 of the Constitution, which emphasize the necessity of respecting the freedom of citizens and the equality of rights between men and women. The last part of Article 9 states that no authority has the right to deprive legitimate freedoms, even though laws and regulations are in place, to preserve the country's independence and territorial integrity.

Furthermore, this verdict has completely disregarded the important principle of "narrow interpretation in favor of the accused," a fundamental principle recognized globally and in various legal systems. In this verdict, the relevant judge not only interpreted the concept of "religious hijab" broadly but also applied an expansive interpretation in attributing multiple charges to the defendant, attributing all charges related to the issue of *unveiledness* to the defendant.

If we accept the judge's broad interpretation, the detrimental result would be that in any single crime, the judge could attribute multiple similar charges found in the law to the accused, contrary to legal principles.

So, after the notification of the verdict mentioned above and prior to the appellate court hearing, I was arrested on similar charges of "encouragement of corruption" and six other charges, and my colleague took over the defense of the defendant in the appeal court.

At this stage of the defense, while emphasizing the legal equality of men and women in their choice of attire, it was also emphasized that attributing three charges to a single act is legally unacceptable. Ultimately, the appellate judge accepted this argument and sentenced Narges Hosseini to a fine.

Naturally, as her lawyer, I fought for her acquittal, but the course of the case did not align well with judicial standards. I was in Evin Prison when the appellate court's ruling was issued, but it was never delivered to me after I was suddenly transferred to Qarchak Prison.

Shaparak Shajari Zadeh

Between December 2017 and March 2018, Shaparak Shajari Zadeh stood in various neighborhoods of Tehran without a headscarf and published her photos on social media. Her method of practicing civil disobedience was similar to that of the other Girls of Revolution Street. Although she had not done it on Enghelab Street itself, like others, she had stood on a raised platform and waved her headscarf on a stick.

Luckily, Shaparak was able to dodge arrest a few times, but because she knew the arrest was inevitable, she had granted me power of attorney ahead of time. On February 21, 2018, she was arrested on Qeitarieh Street without a headscarf. Immediately after her arrest, she went on a hunger strike. As soon as her husband posted bail and she was temporarily released, she called me.

One thing about her that struck me was her ability to articulate her suffering and her intentions in simple language. She never needed to resort to complicated ideological discussion or political discourse to say how compulsory hijab bothered her. Years later and living in exile, Shaparak wrote that after a lifetime of experiencing the regime's stifling control over women's bodies, she finally felt empowered by defying the law and removing her headscarf. She said, "I was an ordinary woman, partaking in an extraordinary movement."

The harassment and arrests did not deter Shaparak. Two months later, during a trip to Kashan City, she once again published a photo of herself without a headscarf in one of the parks in Kashan. She was arrested by the Kashan prosecutor's office. At the time of this writing in 2023, she has two cases related to her act of unveiling.

Charges. Shaparak Shajari Zadeh faced the same three charges in both cases:

1. Encouragement of corruption.
2. Committing a forbidden act.
3. Failure to observe religious hijab.

Both cases were consolidated and referred to Branch 1089 of Criminal Court Two in the Judiciary Complex of Ershad, presided over by Judge Ali Asghar Mousavi Konti, who was also handling the case of Narges Hosseini.

My defense, in this case, was similar to what I used in the previous case. It was based on respect for citizens' freedom, equal rights between men and women, and legal arguments that women are not obliged to observe wearing the hijab in the sense of covering their hair.

In the verdict issued in the case under document number 97099721224400536 on March 22, 2018, the judge ruled the following:

> The defendant, based on the charges of promoting corruption in Tehran and Kashan by uncovering her hijab and removing her headscarf completely in public places, and by standing on a utility box and displaying it on a stick, is sentenced to endure two counts of ten years of imprisonment, with the suspension of the execution of the punishment for eighteen years of imprisonment (to be served for two years) for five years.

Analysis of the issued judgment. For the crime of being unveiled, the judge charged Shaparak with encouragement of corruption, which was not proportionate to her actions.

Furthermore, this verdict contradicts the provisions of Article 134 of the Islamic Penal Code, which states that the harshest punishment should be executed when determining multiple sentences.

Moreover, in the second accusation, the judge considered the act of posting an Instagram photo without a hijab in a park a crime. Even according to the same hijab law, publishing photos and videos of unveiled women is not a crime nor punishable. Nevertheless, the government has been going beyond the confines of this law for years by exploiting its official power and further restricting women.

On June 13, 2018, one day after the court's decision, I had not officially received the verdict when I was arrested at my home. While I was in prison, on July 1, 2018, the Tehran prosecutor at the time was interviewed and, without mentioning Shaparak Shajari Zadeh by name, stated, "One of the Girls of Revolution Street has been sentenced to twenty years in prison."

On July 10, 2018, I wrote a letter to him from Evin Prison and somehow managed to publish it. In it, while referring to the verdict (one to two years of suspended imprisonment), I mentioned that the judiciary has become a tool for creating terror and fear among people. Then, referring to the acid attack on women in Isfahan, I wrote, "Mr. Prosecutor! The public is astonished by the judiciary's reaction to unveiled women and its heavy silence regarding acid attackers and aggressors . . .

Now, tell your judges to increase the number of years they sentence women to prison, condemn women to harsher measures, and keep using foul language. It will yield no result. Because women have decided to assert their authority over their bodies, and our men also realize your oppressive behavior insults their dignity and willpower." And at the end, I asked, "By the way, Mr. Prosecutor, what do your children think about your statements? Do you know? Have you ever asked them?"

The main motivation behind writing this letter was to protest the intimidating atmosphere the prosecutor intended to create through that interview. My client, Shaparak, had left Iran months before my detention. I was certain that when the prosecutor made that statement, he had full knowledge of my client's migration. As her lawyer, I thought I should write such a letter to the prosecutor to support Shaparak's civil rights, the right to free movement and travel, and the right to civil disobedience.

I often took such actions because legal work did not always yield results. Very early on, I learned I had to expand the legal discourse through interviews and raise public awareness. With this approach, I intended to promote a more legal and just perspective toward the defendants and contribute to advancing democracy in Iranian society by fostering a culture of respect for the rights of others, regardless of their beliefs. I believed (and still do) that only under the shelter of such a culture could Iranians experience a peaceful collective life.

My Legal Case

On June 13, 2018, I was arrested after four months of defending the Girls of Revolution Street. Four male and one female officer came to my house. When they came to arrest me, after showing me the arrest warrant, I firmly held on to the apartment door and said that only one of them could go inside. They sent the female officer into the house, and I closed the door behind her. I did this because usually, when they went to someone's house for an arrest, they would all rush inside together and take control of the entire house, including managing and controlling the premises. For example, their other colleagues who were outside would ring the bell, and they would open the door and come in as if it was their own home, freely moving in and out.

The officers had come to our apartment with the arrest warrant to execute a five-year sentence that I had previously received on charges of "conspiracy and collusion to disturb national security." Those five years of imprisonment were for my participation (alongside several other citizens) in a protest against the suspension of my lawyer's license between September 2014 and July 2015 in front of the Bar Association of the Central Judiciary. My protest, which lasted almost nine months, was against the three-year suspension of my law practice license, which was issued by the Disciplinary Court of Lawyers. As soon as the protest began, various individuals joined the protest daily.

They asked me to change, so I deliberately chose a coat with a button that said, "I oppose the mandatory hijab." My husband, Reza Khandan, and one of our close friends, Dr. Farhad Meysami, had spent weeks making thousands of these buttons in support of the Girls of Revolution Street movement. Two months after me, Reza and Farhad were arrested on a similar set of charges, almost all the buttons were confiscated and destroyed, and they were each sentenced to six years in prison.

From the time we first met, Reza has always been a firm supporter of full rights for women and for people of all faiths and backgrounds. We have walked together in life as parents and human rights activists. That's why I love him and have been praising him for thirty years.

As I was leaving the house with the officers, I noticed one of them was recording me on his mobile phone. I asked him to stop, but he didn't, so I picked up my camera from the table and told him that I would do the same to him. At that moment, his supervisor, an elderly man, asked him to stop filming, which he did. These petty intimidations are common among Iranian intelligence; however, over the years, I have learned that their tactics are empty threats. That's why I always make a point to stand up to them.

The officers had taken a taxi to come to pick me up. One of them was having a conversation with the driver about his son, who lived in Sweden. When we reached the gates of Evin Prison, and I was about to get out of the car, I told the driver that all of us, including him, must fight for a better society so our children don't end up migrating to the West.

As soon as I arrived at Evin Courthouse, I was given new charges (on top of the abovementioned charges), including incitement to corruption, conspiracy and collusion, and obscenity. The interrogator angrily read the indictment and demanded that I choose a defense lawyer from a list of pre-approved names.

"I will not defend myself without the presence of my chosen lawyer," I said, because I was well aware that under a law recently passed by the Parliament, only lawyers approved by the judiciary had the right to defend political prisoners and defendants. Clearly, such lawyers were not independent, and I had no intention of using their services.

As part of the new charges with which they had just surprised me, I also received a temporary detention order. Now, I was being transferred to the prison with two warrants.

I was taken to the women's ward of Evin Prison. I knew this place well. I had been an inmate for over three years, starting in 2010, and I've represented many men and women who have been incarcerated there. Evin houses around 15,000 people and has been a center of torture, death, and despair since its construction in 1972.

After a few weeks, I was summoned to the courthouse. I knew it was for the new case. I went to the courthouse but did not engage with anyone; instead, I removed my headscarf and left the room where the interrogation was taking place.

After this, I received several summons to the courthouse but refrained from attending them. However, the case proceeded to court with the issuance of an indictment. I did not participate in the court hearing either.

I did not defend myself because I saw no point in being part of their sham trial, especially since I was denied the right to appoint a lawyer. Plus, the accusations were so numerous and absurd that there was no opportunity for a fair defense. For example, the interrogator accused me of assisting in establishing a home church. Because apostasy in Iran can sometimes be punishable by death, Christian converts born into Muslim families, fearing being caught, are often forced to gather in private homes or secret locations to perform religious rituals. Many people who host religious gatherings at their homes are arrested on charges of establishing home churches.

The accusation was utter nonsense and a blatant lie, so I said, "I wish I had," and added, "I always wanted to have the opportunity to show my solidarity with Christian and Assyrian countrymen and women under pressure."

Later, this accusation was dropped from my case.

Charges. The final indictment included the following charges:

1. Conspiracy and collusion to commit crimes against national security.

2. Propaganda activities against the regime.
3. Active membership in the unlawful group LEGAM (Step-by-Step to Stop the Death Penalty) and Shora-ye-Solh (Peace Council).
4. Encouraging and enabling corruption and obscenity.
5. Disturbance of public order and peace.
6. Spreading false information to manipulate public minds.
7. Appearing without hijab in the interrogations.

Court verdict. These charges were explicitly stated and confirmed in the judgment of Branch 28 of the Revolutionary Court under case number 97/28/150, dated November 3, 2018.

> Regarding the charges against Ms. Nasrin Sotoudeh, including conspiracy and collusion to commit crimes against national security, propaganda activities against the regime, effective membership in an unlawful group against the government, encouragement of corruption and obscenity and providing the means for their occurrence, disturbance of public order and tranquility, spreading false information with the intention to manipulate public minds, and appearing without observing the required religious hijab, considering the contents of the case file and the conducted investigations, as well as the report of the Ministry of Intelligence, it is established that the defendant, in collaboration and

collusion with key antirevolutionary elements inside and outside the country, following the disturbances in December 2017 protests, published a statement and requested the holding of a referendum under the supervision of the United Nations organization was involved in determining the type of government. Together with Shirin Ebadi, a member of the hidden group of human rights defenders, Narges Mohammadi, the deputy head of the Center for Human Rights Defenders, Payam Akhavan, Jafar Panahi, Mohsen Sazegara, Mohammad Saifzadeh, Hassan Shariatmadari, Hashem Shabaz-Zadeh, Abolfazl Ghadiani, Mohsen Kadhivar, Kazem Kardavani, Mohsen Makhmalbaf, Mohammad Maleki, and Mohammad Nourizad, all of them individuals who oppose and seek to overthrow the Islamic Republic system, some of whom are in hiding outside the country and some inside, have signed and supported a statement released by the accused and have pursued the plan of overthrowing the Islamic Republic system using the keyword "referendum" and have continued their activities. One of their activities includes numerous interviews with foreign media outlets against the Islamic Republic.

After the Girls of Revolution Street protested against the compulsory hijab and unveiled in public, the accused, to promote corruption and obscenity in society, published a video of herself on social media in which she supported the illegal actions of these individuals by unveiling herself. The accused then, in collaboration with her husband Reza Khandan and some members of the movement to overthrow the government, went to the location where the Girls of Revolution Street unveiled themselves and placed a bouquet of flowers on the utility box and distributed buttons with the slogan, "I object to compulsory hijab," to encourage and persuade people to remove their hijab in public. The accused participated in an unlawful gathering of Gonabadi Dervishes on January 9, 2018, and on October 9, 2017, together with members of the illegal group LEGAM, she organized an unlawful gathering in front of the United Nations office and delivered a speech. On September 7, 2017, she participated in an illegal gathering against the Islamic Republic system in front of Evin Prison.

Considering the contents of the case and the conducted investigations, the allegations against the accused are substantiated. The court, regarding the charges of conspiracy and collusion to commit crimes against national security, in accordance with Article 610 of the Islamic Penal Code, sentences the accused to seven years and six months of imprisonment. Regarding propaganda activities against the regime, per Article 500 of the Islamic Penal Code, the accused is sentenced to one year and six months of imprisonment, considering the days already spent in detention. Regarding effective membership in the unlawful group LEGAM, per Article 499 of the Islamic Penal Code, the accused is sentenced to seven years and six months of imprisonment, taking into account the days already spent in detention. Regarding the encouragement of corruption and obscenity, in accordance with Article 639 of the Islamic Penal Code, the accused is sentenced to twelve years of imprisonment, taking into account the days already spent in detention.

Regarding appearing without hijab in public, per Article 638 of the Islamic Penal Code, the accused is sentenced to seventy-four lashes. Regarding spreading false information intending to manipulate the public, per Article 698 of the Islamic Penal Code, the accused is sentenced to three years of imprisonment and seventy-four lashes. Regarding disturbance of public order, in accordance with Article 618 of the Islamic Penal Code, the accused is sentenced to two years of imprisonment, taking into account the days already spent in detention.

The verdict is issued in absentia and can be appealed within twenty days from the date of notification at this court, and after that, it can be subject to review at the provincial appellate courts. Article 134 of the Islamic Penal Code applies in this case.

Analysis of the court verdict. The court referred to several of my various activities, including the following:

1. Requesting, along with other civil activists, a referendum for the establishment of an alternative government. Our statement said in part, "The only way out of the current situation is a peaceful transition from an Islamic Republic toward a secular state based on parliamentary democracy and free people's votes, which fully respects human rights, eliminates all institutionalized discrimination, particularly against women, ethnic and religious minorities, and all other minorities."

2. Advocating for the rights of the Girls of Revolution Street.

3. Membership in the group called Laghve Gam be Gam or LEGAM (Step-by-Step to Stop the Death Penalty) that campaigned against executions. This campaign was initiated in 2013 by the poet Simin Behbahani, activist Parvin Fahimi (her son was killed in the 2009 protests), defense attorney Babak Ahmadi, former president of the University of Tehran Mohammad Maleki, filmmaker and activist Mohammad Nourizad, economist Fariborz Raeis-Dana, journalist Alireza Jabbari, Kurdish activist Esmail Mofazzadeh, and renowned filmmaker Jafar Panahi. Later, the activist Narges Mohammadi and I joined as well. In its declaration statement, the campaign proposed solutions for the abolition of executions in Iran and stated that in the first step, its focus is on abolishing the execution of

juveniles under eighteen, political prisoners, public executions, and stoning.
4. Gathering in front of the United Nations office to mark World Day Against the Death Penalty.
5. Distributing the button with the slogan, "I am against the mandatory hijab."
6. Participating in a demonstration in front of Evin Prison.
7. Appearing without proper Islamic hijab at the place of interrogation.

Additional charges sentenced me to thirty-three-and-a-half years in prison plus 148 lashes. Later, the prison authorities informed me that the previous five-year prison sentence was also executable, thus increasing the total sentence against me to thirty-eight-and-a-half years.

In Iran, prisoners never receive an official list of sentences. Worse, sentences can easily increase from time to time because there is no supervision or proof of verdict for prisoners to use. So, when I was told what my sentences were, I immediately asked for a piece of paper so that I could write everything down word by word. They agreed.

As soon as I came across the words thirty-three years in prison and 148 lashes, I thought about my nineteen-year-old daughter, Mehraveh, and eleven-year-old son, Nima. Even though I had no fear of prison or lashing, I wondered how I was going to explain such a horrible concept as lashing to a child. I was torn because I didn't want to hide things from them, either. It took me almost ten days to even tell my husband, Reza, and even longer to tell Nima and Mehraveh.

Both Reza and I tried to act calmly and confidently around the kids. At home, Reza made sure there wasn't going to be any interruption in their meals (he became a good cook), school, and extracurricular activities such as the art and music classes they took all year round.

In order to act normally about life in prison, we both had to adopt the attitude of normality. We couldn't fake it and expect our kids not to pick up on it. Because we both went on with our daily lives and activism with a positive attitude, I was able to meet Mehraveh and Nima in prison and be brave and happy around them. I refused to acknowledge the legitimacy of these charges and refrained from any defense or appeal. Approximately two years after the verdict was issued, Branch 28 of the Revolutionary Court, based on the new Reduction of Retributive Penalties law, reduced my imprisonment sentence to twenty-three years, with ten years executable in the initial stage. The sentence of flogging was also removed in the new verdict.

Since April 20, 2021, when I was granted a medical furlough for a heart angioplasty and a case of COVID-19 that I caught in Qarchak Prison, I have been home.

Like many prisoners, I often asked myself whether what I did was worth being in prison and away from my family. As a lawyer, despite knowing the risks of being a human rights lawyer in Iran, I sometimes questioned my motivation for pursuing legal work and exposing myself and my family to danger, threats, and years of being apart. At the same time, I found ways to prevent prison from being too painful. I reflected on those who had been imprisoned before me, such as Shirin Ebadi, Mehrangiz Kar, Abdolfattah Soltani, and many other lawyers who had been jailed for defending the rights of citizens.

In 2010, when I was first detained and kept in solitary confinement at the Ministry of Intelligence detention center, I thought about the infamous Her Majesty's Prison Maze in Northern Ireland. I had visited it a few years before during a trip to Ireland. I was five months pregnant with my son, Nima, at the time. It was a terrifying prison that had been turned into a museum. One of the rooms was the cell of Bobby Sands, a member of the Provisional Irish Republican Army who lost his life at twenty-seven after a sixty-six-day hunger strike in 1981. Sitting in my cell, I would think, "If Bobby Sands could endure that prison for his demands, I can too." I had to endure, just as many before me had done, and many were doing all around me.

I hope someday Evin Prison will be turned into a museum.

The thought of many great nonviolent fighters kept me strong and hopeful in prison. Martin Luther King Jr. wrote from the Birmingham jail, "I am here because injustice exists." I constantly told myself what is extraordinary is the blatant injustice that exists in revolutionary courts. These courts violated important legal principles, the court sessions were dominated by interrogators and security forces that did not belong there, and the defendants and their lawyers were constantly threatened. Breathing in such an unjust environment was difficult. Surely, no one should embrace going to prison, but I was (and I am) willing to do it because, as long as there is injustice in my society, I will fight it.

Two weeks after my arrest in 2010, my father died in the hospital, but I was not allowed to attend his funeral. Being unable to say goodbye to him or do my duty as a daughter who should perform her father's last rite filled me with sadness and sometimes even anger.

A few months after his passing, I looked forward to reading the newspaper given to prisoners daily. In those days, *Ettela'at,* Iran's largest conservative paper, published Nelson Mandela's book *Long Walk to Freedom* in short installments. I was looking forward to the excerpt but was not expecting what I began to read. Mandela was talking about the death of his mother when he was on Robben Island and not being allowed to go to her funeral.

I felt Mandela was talking to me. I felt Mandela's words had reached me in my cell for a reason. It reminded me that others have endured similar hardships. Others have fought and missed out on milestones and important events in their lives and in the lives of their loved ones too. All of that was for the sake of justice and democracy. That's how I knew my time in prison was worth it.

Conclusion

In *The Handmaid's Tale*, Margaret Atwood demonstrates how mothers play a significant role in shaping the destinies of their daughters in an autocratic society like Iran. The well-being and safety of their daughters are a priority to them. Atwood's mothers might seem cruel at times, but the reader knows they have no choice but to be strict in order to keep their children safe. I remember summers when young girls and their mothers argued over the length of school uniforms at the tailors before returning to school in the fall. Fortunately or unfortunately, I never experienced this with my mother since, despite being devout, she believed in my freedom to choose. But this did not mean that I was unaware of my surroundings. The young girls wanted shorter uniforms, while mothers wanted to adhere to the dress code. They wished to spare their children the hassle of trouble with school authorities and morality police.

In my generation, many women (myself included) decided not to challenge our daughters over small matters like the length of a dress or a scarf. However, we did not realize giving our children freedom would later expose them to harm and harassment.

However, open-minded mothers long before the 1979 revolution have always lived in Iran. They coexisted with the more traditional women. The liberal-minded women emphasized the importance of women's economic independence, employment, and higher education. They empowered young women on both the personal level by educating their daughters and on the national level by pushing for programs that empowered young girls and women. And their numbers were not insignificant.

For this reason, men who were very well aware of this and hoped to create an Islamic government (which had not yet come to power) could not explicitly reveal their plans to confine women to homes or basic gender-appropriate jobs. Instead, they advocated for mandatory hijab by disguising it as a matter of morality and Islamic identity. In my opinion, this laid the foundation for depriving women's rights in every sphere.

As a lawyer, I have witnessed blatant injustice and unimaginable suffering. In one instance, a thirteen-year-old girl in the northern city of Rasht was sentenced to death by execution for murder. A student who had participated in student protests and happened to be in prison for it brought her plight to my attention at Evin. She spent her childhood and the best years of her life under the shadow of execution and twice endured torture in prison. Even though the death sentence had been finalized, my efforts finally paid off thanks to numerous civic activists who fought alongside me. She was freed after spending twenty years in prison. Her suffering resulted from a law that deemed girls criminally responsible at nine years old. Her case, like many others involving murder, was plagued with numerous ambiguities that failed to prove her guilt. In this particular case, the court issued the death penalty based on the coerced confession of a thirteen-year-old girl against herself.

In another example, I—once again, with several other civil activists—managed to secure the release of an individual with the victim's family's consent. This was possible because, according to the Islamic Penal Code, in *qisas* (retribution) for murder, the *diyah* (blood money) can be paid to the victim's immediate family to waive the right to *qisas*.

After the revolution, horrific stories about the government enforcing mandatory hijab for women emerged. The slogan, "Either the headscarf or a beating, we've been summoned," illustrated instances of acid attacks, fear of losing jobs, and other situations that placed women in vulnerable positions.

I also remember two young relatives in the northwestern city of Tabriz. Dressed up and carefree, they were going to a friend's party when two police officers on a motorcycle threw paint on the young girls. Shaken and frightened, thinking it was acid, they had to return home, their party ruined. In the example of my relatives, their parents helped them clean up and consoled them because there was no other option. Who could they have possibly turned to? Which police station could they have complained to?

That's why women thought their movement should start exactly where the injustice had begun; the harassment of women!

This viewpoint, which existed in every Iranian woman's mind, found a wide reflection through the Girls of Revolution Street movement against compulsory hijab. The protest aimed to challenge the imposition of mandatory hijab and bring down the commanding hands of oppressive men. Many men stood alongside them because they were tired of such injustice and inequality toward women. They knew that happiness could not be achieved without justice and equality. That's why many men joined the street girls' movement in various cities. They would climb onto electric poles in their towns, tie a feminine scarf to a branch, and wave it in the air.

Among my clients, some men were pursued due to their participation in civil disobedience. They had come to my office to seek legal representation, but unfortunately, I was arrested before I could begin defending them.

The retelling of these stories and the oppressive control exerted by the government over women's bodies gradually confronted women's minds with the bitter reality that we would never have equal power to negotiate or achieve our desires through the imposition of the hijab.

Women would take to the streets to protest against the discrimination of their rights and engage in various campaigns, but they would easily be detained.

It was at this point, after the dimming of the women's movement, that the Girls of Revolution Street movement emerged through their individual actions, and five years later, with the state-sanctioned killing of Mahsa Amini for her hijab, a movement called Women, Life, Freedom took shape. It responded to forty-four years of disrespect toward women, their rights, and their bodies. These were three slogans that the Islamic government preferred to suppress.

The Girls of Revolution Street movement was also suppressed after three months. The lives of many of them became intertwined with such pressures that they were forced to leave their homeland.

Many of those who, like me, have chosen to engage in human rights activities through legal representation and defense of political prisoners and civil activists have suffered stories similar to those I have described. We, human rights activists who have chosen this path, believe that establishing a fair judicial system could contribute to creating democracy in society. The existence of a fair judicial system also responds to an inherent need for equality in living within a society. However, the most important characteristic of a fair judicial system is its independence from the government. In this case, the power of such a judicial system lies in its ability to address the misconduct of individuals within the government, those who have engaged in financial corruption, or those who have neglected their duties or violated the freedoms and rights of individuals in societies like ours through abuse of their governmental positions.

For this reason, many lawyers, including myself, took on the defense of politically or civilly active individuals who faced political charges. I selected two examples of legal cases for investigation in this essay, in addition to my own case, totaling three examples, to carefully examine the judicial weaknesses in handling these cases, which are significant. I intended to prevent the repetition of such proceedings in the future system we all hope for. Otherwise, if the current judicial system continues to replicate political animosity and hostility, we will never find ourselves on the path to democracy; a prerequisite for democracy, above all, is the existence of judicial security for citizens through fair trials.

When I work, defend my clients, go to court to advocate for them, and end up in prison, I certainly think about the future. I think about a future where no particular class holds absolute power over a society based on gender, race, religion, or any other reason. In this way, we not only teach equality to our children but also remind them and ourselves that no one has the right to dictate their freedom based on gender, religion, or race. Instead, when choosing such methods, we learn how to achieve equality without hatred and violence for ourselves and future generations.

We can't talk about civil movements without drawing from the valuable experiences of figures like Martin Luther King Jr., Václav Havel, Nelson Mandela, or Mahatma Gandhi, who said, "The true measure of any society can be found in how it treats its most vulnerable members." Their leadership brought substantial change to their respective countries. They also felt a responsibility to reduce the risk of violence, without sacrificing their goals.

The future lies in the methods we employ to challenge a government based on various inequalities. If we are to replace such a government using similar techniques, we will end up with a regime identical to the current one. However, if we assume responsibility for every citizen's life and learn from nonviolent movements, we can create a different government and transform the current political system. This new system would provide space for diverse social groups to express themselves and thrive, all within the framework of the law.

I am not concerned about being labeled either too timid or too bold. I am deeply concerned about the increasing number of casualties and harm inflicted upon individuals. While I fear the continuation of the tyrannical rule, we therefore need a vision to break our society's oppression cycle. I believe that the Girls of Revolution Street movement has shed light on this path to a certain extent by choosing a nonviolent and courageous approach. Despite being subjected to physical and judicial attacks, the girls refrained from seeking revenge but continued their movement to the extent that Women, Life, Freedom emerged from the ashes. Each time such a window of opportunity appears, it can only be opened through nonviolence. One of the most important tools to overcome this tyranny is the law. Only the law can establish a fair judiciary for both dissenters and supporters within our society.

As I mentioned in the description of the judicial proceedings related to the Women, Life, Freedom protestors, some chose to stay in Iran, while others were forced to leave their homeland. However, regardless of their choices, handling their cases lacked the characteristics of a fair trial. These cases were influenced by political dynamics intertwined with an irrational obsession over women's veiling, leading to biased rulings. Nonetheless, it has been one of the most shining experiences in the civil rights struggles for equality and justice, a movement that managed to capture the attention of diverse social strata both within and without the country.

I cannot stress this enough: we can never repeat the volume of violence and injustice that has been inflicted upon us. Undoubtedly, repeating such violence would turn us into a new monster. We would once again accumulate our history from another decade, only to leave the next generation, twenty years from now, without an answer. We cannot fill our history with repetitive tales of violence. Our inability to repeat these gruesome stories stems from our desire to be human, to live ordinary lives like people everywhere. We need to reshape our history with love, law, and justice to thrive within that space and live our lives.

Can we remain hopeful about the future, despite the pressures I mentioned and the methods imposed on us over the past forty-four years? This is a question that you, as the reader, have the right to ask me. Will we ultimately triumph over the tyrannical beast that has entrenched itself in the private layers of our lives?

International documents emphasizing our collective commitment to peace and global security stress that these two can be achieved only under respect for human rights. We remember how the United Nations Charter, formulated after World War II, sought to heal the pain and suffering caused by war: "We, the peoples of the United Nations, determined to save succeeding generations from the scourge of war . . . and reaffirming faith in fundamental human rights, in the dignity and worth of the human person, in the equal rights of men and women . . . and to establish conditions under which justice and respect for the obligations arising from treaties and other sources of international law can be maintained . . . and to promote social progress and better standards of life in larger freedom, have resolved to combine our efforts to accomplish these aims."

These concepts have been reiterated in the Universal Declaration of Human Rights, adopted by the United Nations General Assembly several years after the end of

World War II. It states: "Whereas disregard and contempt for human rights have resulted in barbarous acts which have outraged the conscience of mankind, and the advent of a world in which human beings shall enjoy the freedom of speech and belief and freedom from fear and want . . . Whereas the people of the United Nations have reaffirmed their faith in fundamental human rights, in the dignity and worth of the human person, and in the equal rights of men and women, and have determined to promote social progress and better standards of life in larger freedom." Iran signed this agreement under the previous regime, and it is technically still in force.

Given that one of the most important principles of human rights is women's rights, and considering that the observance of fundamental principles such as justice and equality necessitates respect for women's rights, and acknowledging that one of the biggest challenges in Iranian civil society is the violation of women's rights, for these reasons, the realization of international peace and security is contingent upon respecting women's rights. However, the main question is, "Do these rights materialize?"

As I mentioned at the beginning of this chapter, Iranian mothers' mindsets, unfortunately, shape daughters' fates. Mothers who lived in the male-dominated world of that era were influenced by their fathers. Mothers preferred their daughters to be more covered. Mothers separated the spiritual freedom of their daughters from their physical freedom.

Nowadays, the perspectives of many Iranian mothers and fathers have indeed changed. They want their daughters to be able to decide for themselves what they want to wear, think, and do.

Sadly, the current ruling authority refuses to permit this freedom, regardless of the view of its citizens. I believe that when a society's public opinion clearly demands the separation of religion from governance and rejects the ruling authority's interference in various aspects of life, including women's attire, it will inevitably lead to significant change. We are getting closer to this reality. This movement in Iran, like every other movement, experiences ups and downs. However, ultimately, it is the belief of the people that manifests in public life. Therefore, the collective destiny is in our hands. We are obliged to take it.

About the Author

Nasrin Sotoudeh is an Iranian lawyer and human rights activist who has been called "Iran's Nelson Mandela." She is the recipient of the 2023 Brown Democracy Medal from the McCourtney Institute for Democracy, marking the award's tenth year. Sotoudeh has dedicated her legal career to fighting for the rights of women, children, religious and ethnic minorities, journalists and artists, and those facing execution. Her clients include the Nobel Peace Prize laureate Shirin Ebadi, prodemocracy activist Heshmat Tabarzadi, filmmaker Jafar Panahi, and women protesting Iran's mandatory hijab laws. As a result of this advocacy, Sotoudeh has been repeatedly imprisoned by the Iranian government for crimes against the state. She served one sentence from 2010 to 2013 and was sentenced again in 2018 to thirty-eight years and six months in prison and 148 lashes.

Sotoudeh is also a longtime opponent of the death penalty and advocate of improving imprisonment health conditions. She cofounded the organization Step-by-Step to Stop the Death Penalty in 2013 to advocate for legislation that would abolish capital punishment in Iran. In October 2020, Sotoudeh launched a forty-six-day hunger strike to protest poor health conditions and the risk of COVID-19 in Iranian prisons. She is currently on medical leave from prison but could be called back at any time. Most recently in 2022, she received the Robert Badinter Award at the 8th World Congress Against the Death Penalty.

Her work has been featured in the 2020 documentary *Nasrin*, by filmmakers Jeff Kaufman and Marcia S. Ross. Kaufman and Ross have known Sotoudeh since 2016 and are honored to share her story with the Penn State community and accept the Brown Democracy Award on her behalf.

Milton Keynes UK
Ingram Content Group UK Ltd.
UKHW012009150923
428767UK00005B/162